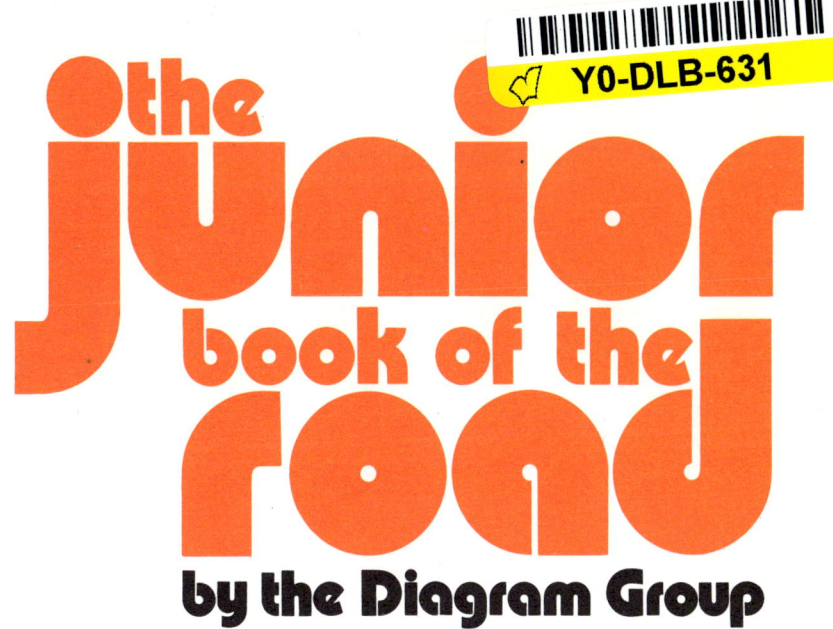

the junior book of the road

by the Diagram Group

Sidgwick & Jackson London

This book has lots of things to look out for on a long car journey. You should be able to enjoy finding them as you travel along, or perhaps when you stop for petrol or for something to eat. Why not keep a log book of your journey and make a note of when and where you spot all the things mentioned in this book?

While you are trying to answer the questions put your hand over the answers.

First published in 1977 by Sidgwick and Jackson Limited
Copyright 1977 by Diagram Visual Information Limited
ISBN 0 283 98383 3
Printed in Great Britain by William Clowes
for Sidgwick and Jackson Limited
1 Tavistock Chambers, Bloomsbury Way
London WC1A 2SG

Watch out!

How many of these things can you spot on your journey today?

Contents

pages	
6-7	The personal touch
8-9	Motorway maze
10-11	Up in the sky
12-13	Roadside animals
14-15	Signs to see
16-17	Travelling by road
18-19	Special buildings
20-21	Know your manufacturer
22-23	Naturalist's notebook
24-25	Get to know a car's inside
26-27	Rolling along
28-29	Strangers ahead
30-31	Joining a club
32-33	Built for the job
34-35	Trees and leaves
36-37	Attention! Men at work
38-39	Plants
40-41	Unusual cargoes
42-43	Birds
44-45	Bridges
46-47	Small creatures

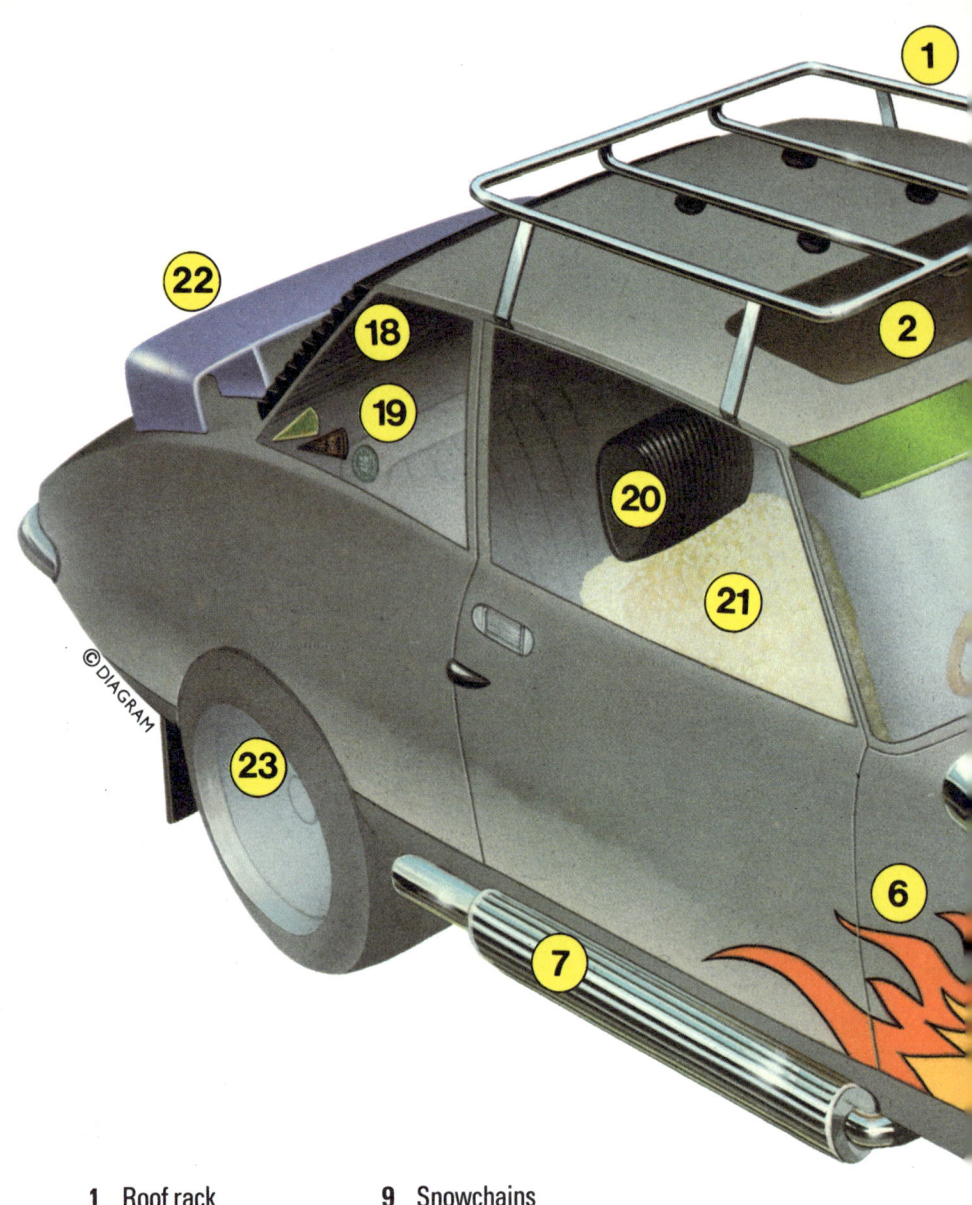

1	Roof rack	9	Snowchains	17	Aerial
2	Sliding roof	10	Fog lamps	18	Louvred window
3	Visor	11	Club badges	19	Holiday stickers
4	Wood steering wheel	12	Maker's badge	20	Head restraint
5	Driving mirror	13	Spot lamp cover	21	Seat cover
6	"Customized" painting	14	Road fund licence	22	Aerofoil
7	Exterior exhaust	15	Parking permit	23	Wide wheels
8	Mud flaps	16	Wiper aerofoils		

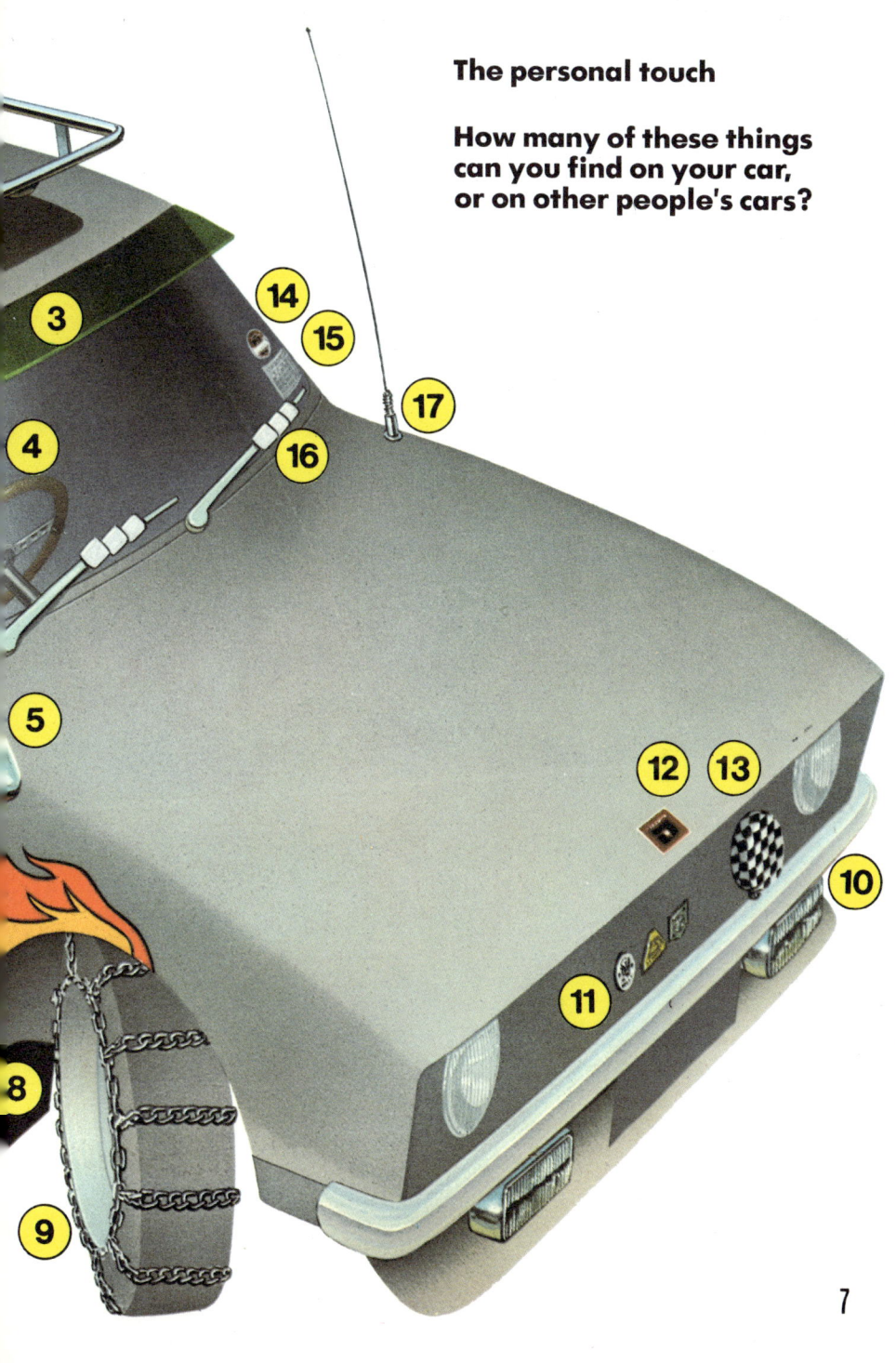

Motorway maze

Your car is about to run out of petrol.

Find the shortest route to the petrol station over or under the bridges — otherwise you'll be stuck!

Up in the sky

The sky is changing all the time. What is it like today?
Can you see an aircraft vapour trail or a rainbow?
Do you know the names of different kinds of clouds?

1	Cirrocumulus
2	Cirrus
3	Aircraft vapour trail
4	Cumulonimbus
5	Altocumulus
6	Cumulus
7	Stratus
8	Nimbostratus
9	Rainbow

Roadside animals

Have you ever seen any of these animals?
Where do you think each of them lives?

1. Mole lives in tunnels marked by molehills **a**
2. Rabbit lives in a warren under the ground **b**
3. Fox lives in other creatures' empty holes **c**
4. Bat sleeps in old buildings **d**
5. Badger lives in a set dug underground **e**
6. Hedgehog lives under dead leaves **f**
7. Squirrel lives in trees **g**
8. Fieldmouse lives in a nest in a cornfield **h**

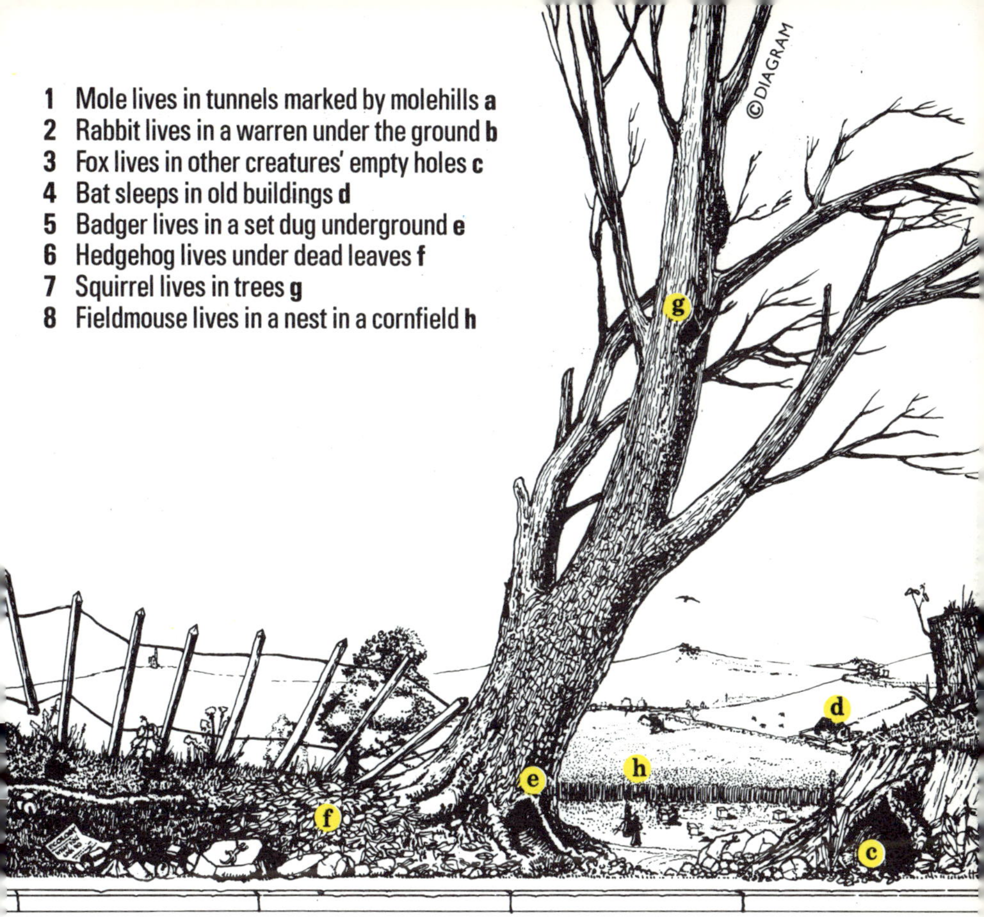

5

6

7

8

Signs to see   How many of these signs can you spot?

11

12

13

14

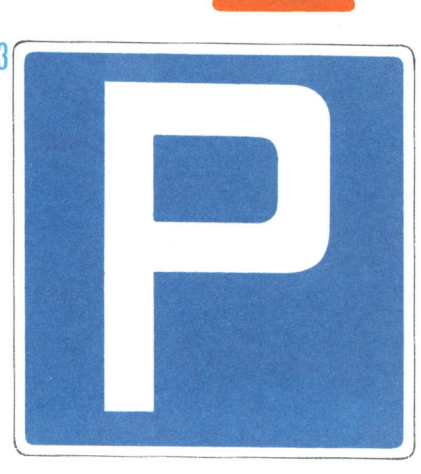

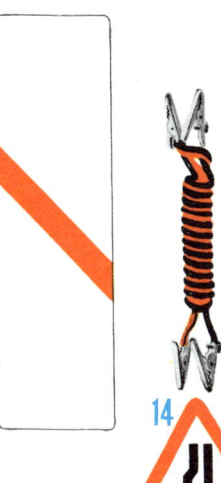

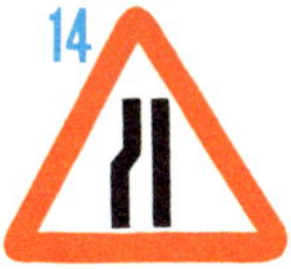

15

1 No entry
2 Quayside or river bank
3 Keep left
4 No stopping
5 Minimum speed limit
6 Steep hill upwards
7 Beware wild animals
8 No through road
9 To public telephone
10 Turn left ahead
11 Markers approaching concealed level crossing
12 Uneven road
13 Parking
14 Road narrows on nearside
15 No left turn

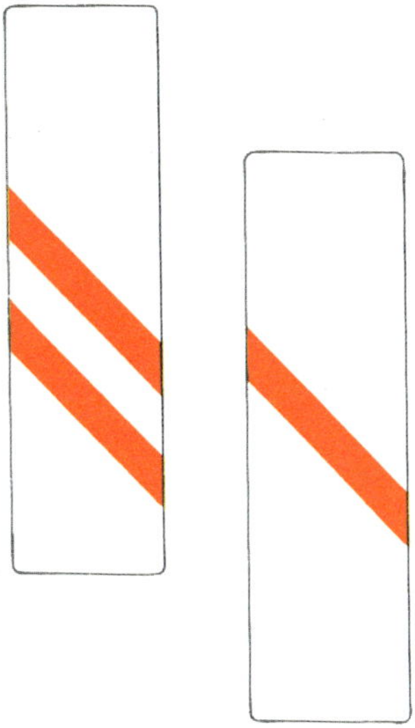

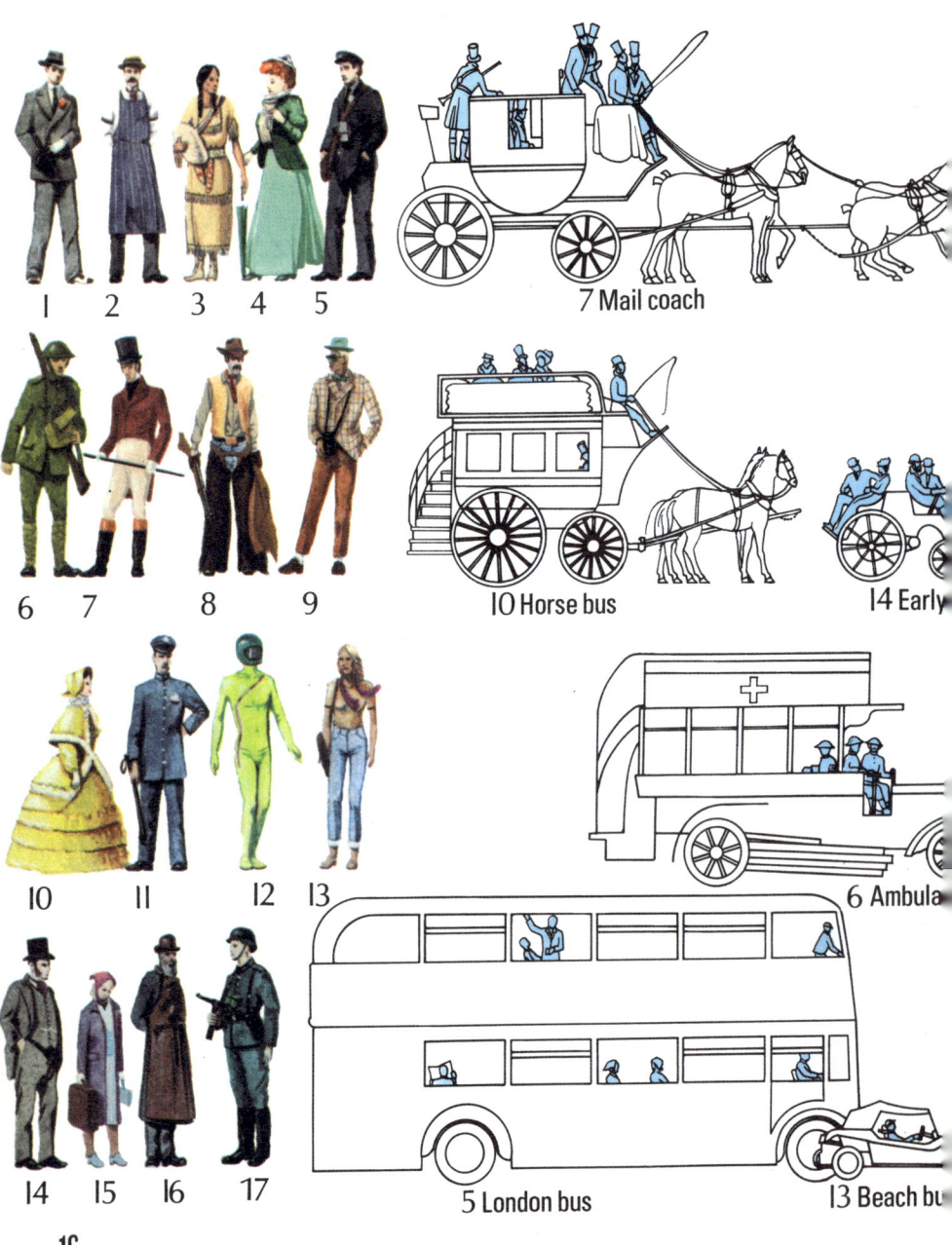

times and places in their own vehicles?

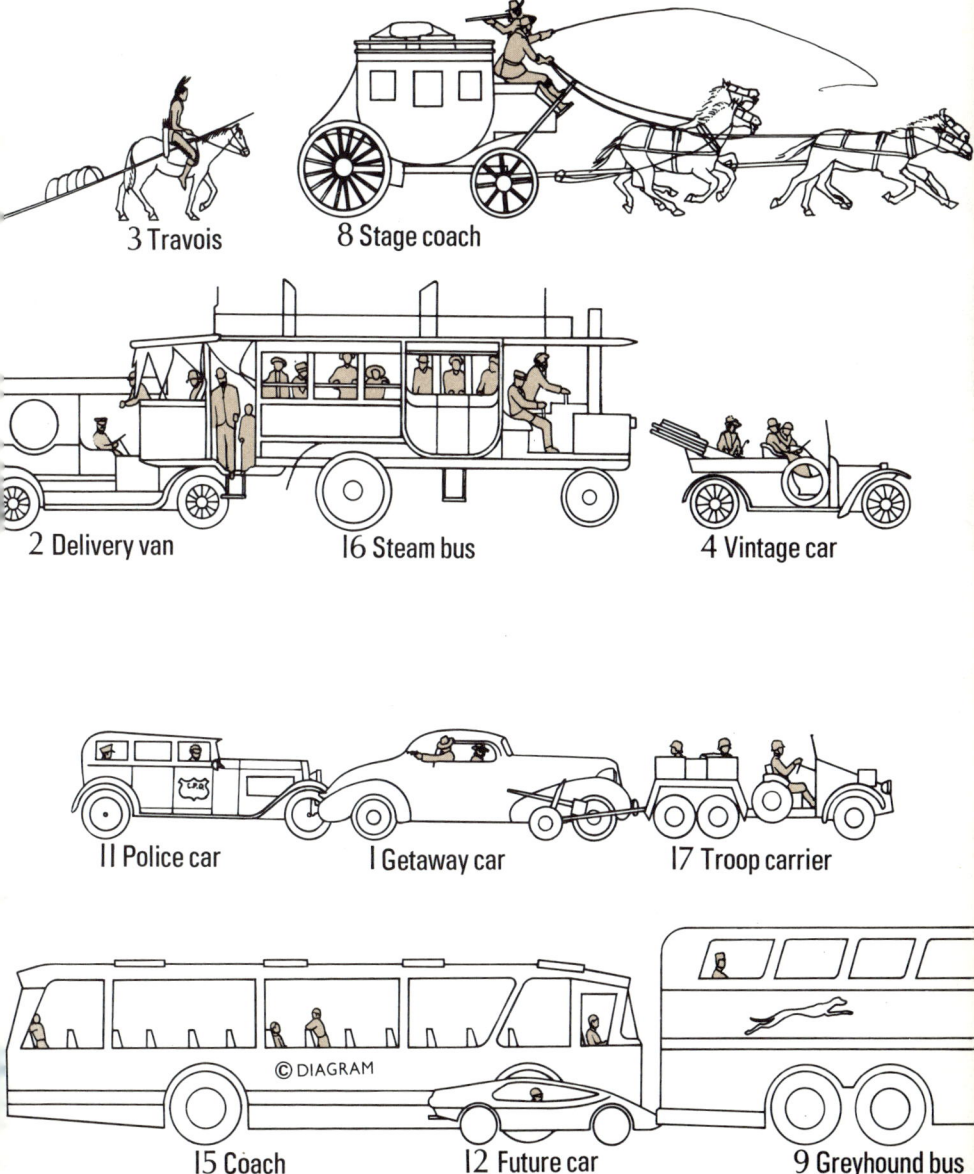

Special buildings

You can see many unusual buildings and structures on a journey. Here are the silhouettes of some of them. Do you know what they are?

1

5

6

9

10

11

16

17

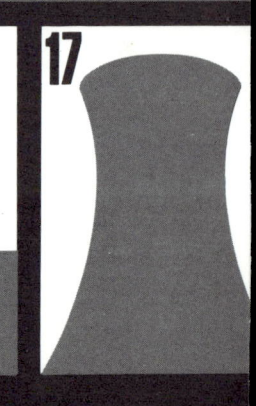

18

1 Block of flats	**8** Oast house	**13** War memorial
2 Power station	**9** Crane	**14** Television mast
3 Statue	**10** Lighthouse	**15** Windmill
4 Ancient stone circle	**11** Head of a coal mine	**16** Aerodrome
5 Cathedral	**12** Dutch barn	**17** Cooling tower
6 Gas cylinder		
7 Castle		

Know your manufacturer

Every firm that makes cars has its own emblem. Do any of these appear on your car? How many others can you find?

1	Morris *(Britain)*
2	Bentley *(Britain)*
3	Lotus *(Britain)*
4	Mercedes-Benz *(Germany)*
5	BMW *(Germany)*
6	Riley *(Britain)*
7	MG *(Britain)*
8	Citroën *(France)*
9	Buick *(USA)*
10	Ford *(USA)*
11	Peugeot *(France)*
12	Volvo *(Sweden)*

Get to know a car's inside

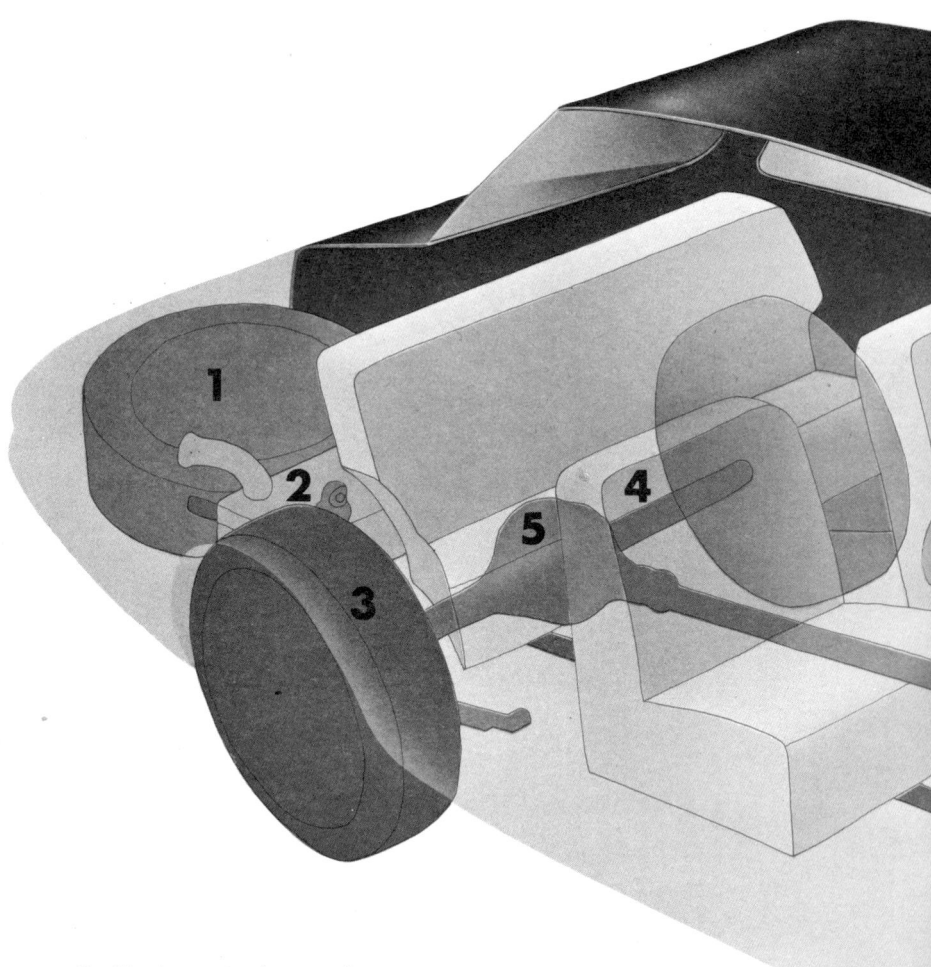

 9   The front wheels steer the car
10   The springs give a smooth ride
11   The brakes stop the car
12   The engine drives the back wheels
13   The radiator keeps the engine cool
14   The clutch pedal helps to change gear
15   The brake pedal controls all the wheels
16   The accelerator pedal makes the engine go faster

These are some of the important parts of a car.

1. The spare wheel is in case of a puncture
2. The petrol tank holds the fuel
3. The back wheels drive the car along
4. The axle joins the rear wheels
5. The drive joins the axle to the engine
6. The steering wheel controls the front wheels
7. The brake lever controls the back wheel brakes
8. The gear shift changes the gear

Rolling along   **Which wheel fits which vehicle?**

1 Army troop carrier has wheel **a**
2 Penny-farthing bicycle has wheel **b**
3 Moon buggy has wheel **c**
4 Veteran car has wheel **d**
5 Chariot has wheel **e**
6 Early railway engine has wheel **f**
7 Ox-drawn cart has wheel **g**
8 Long distance American truck has wheel **h**
9 Road roller has wheel **i**

27

Strangers ahead

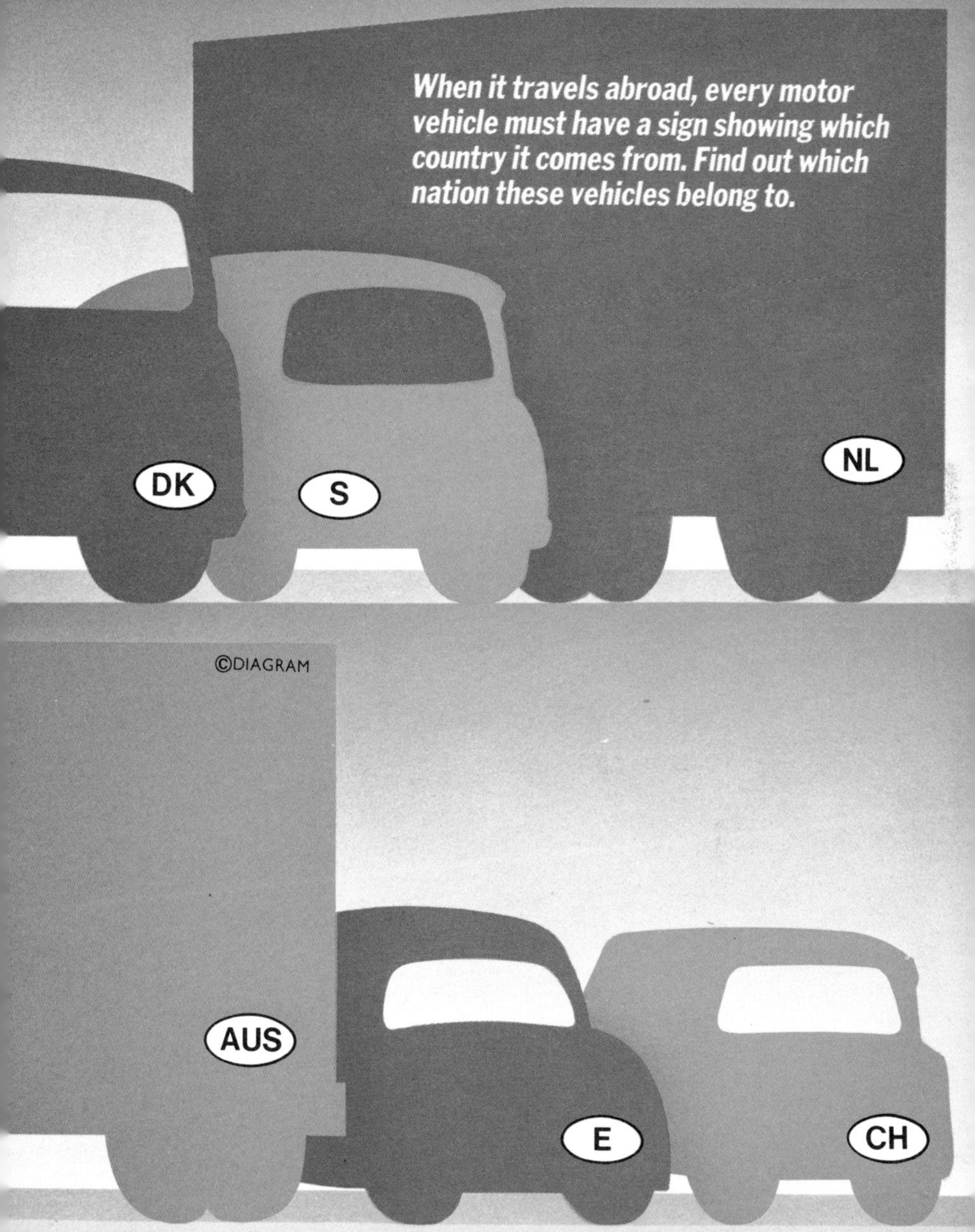

F	France	**USA**	United States of America
D	Germany	**GB**	Great Britain
DK	Denmark	**AUS**	Australia
S	Sweden	**E**	Spain
NL	Netherlands	**CH**	Switzerland

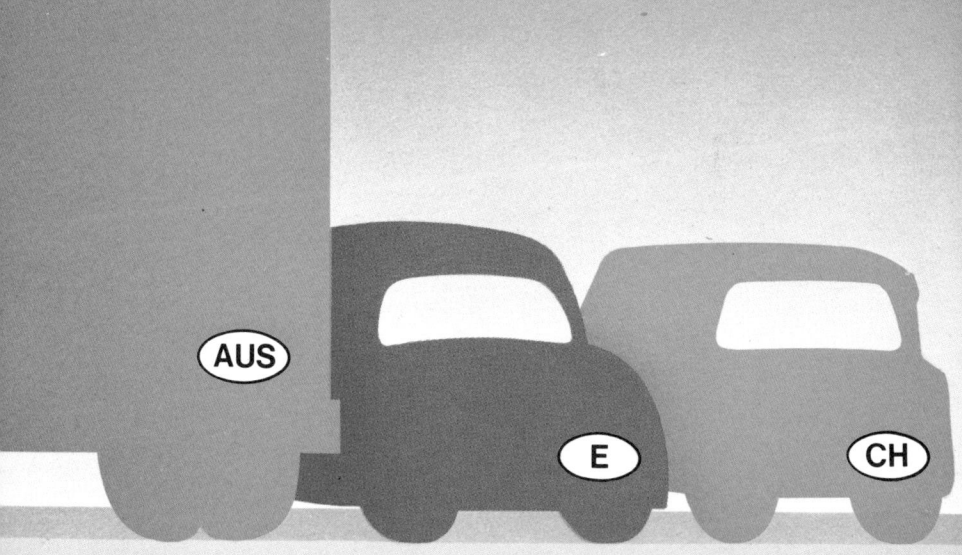

Joining a club

Motorists like joining clubs and collecting badges. How many of these badges can you see? Which are their clubs?

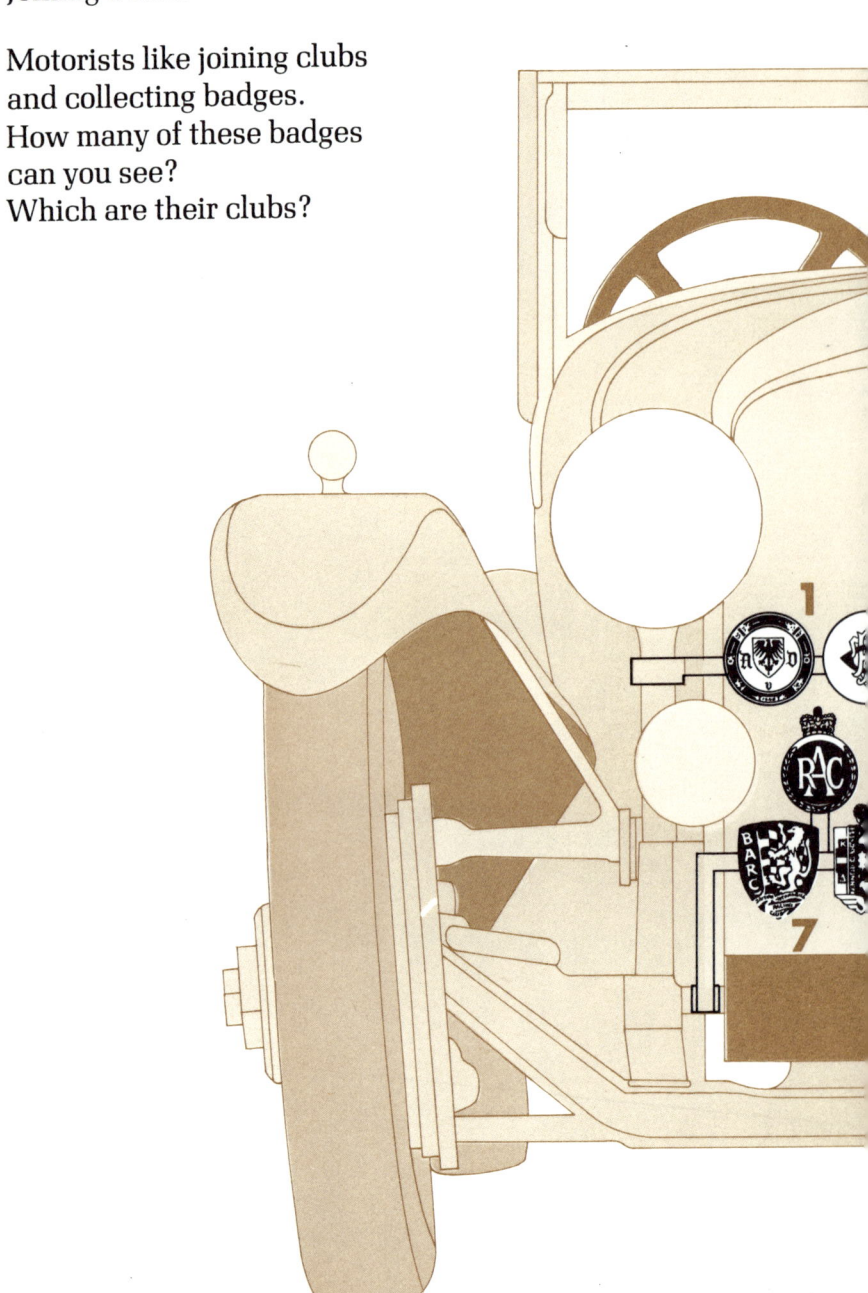

1 Automobilclub von Deutschland
2 Touring Club de France
3 Irish Motor Racing Club
4 Touring Club Italiano
5 Royal Automobile Club
6 Automobile Association
7 British Automobile Racing Club
8 Kooninklijke Nederlandsche Automobiel Club
9 Vintage Sports-car Club
10 American Automobile Association

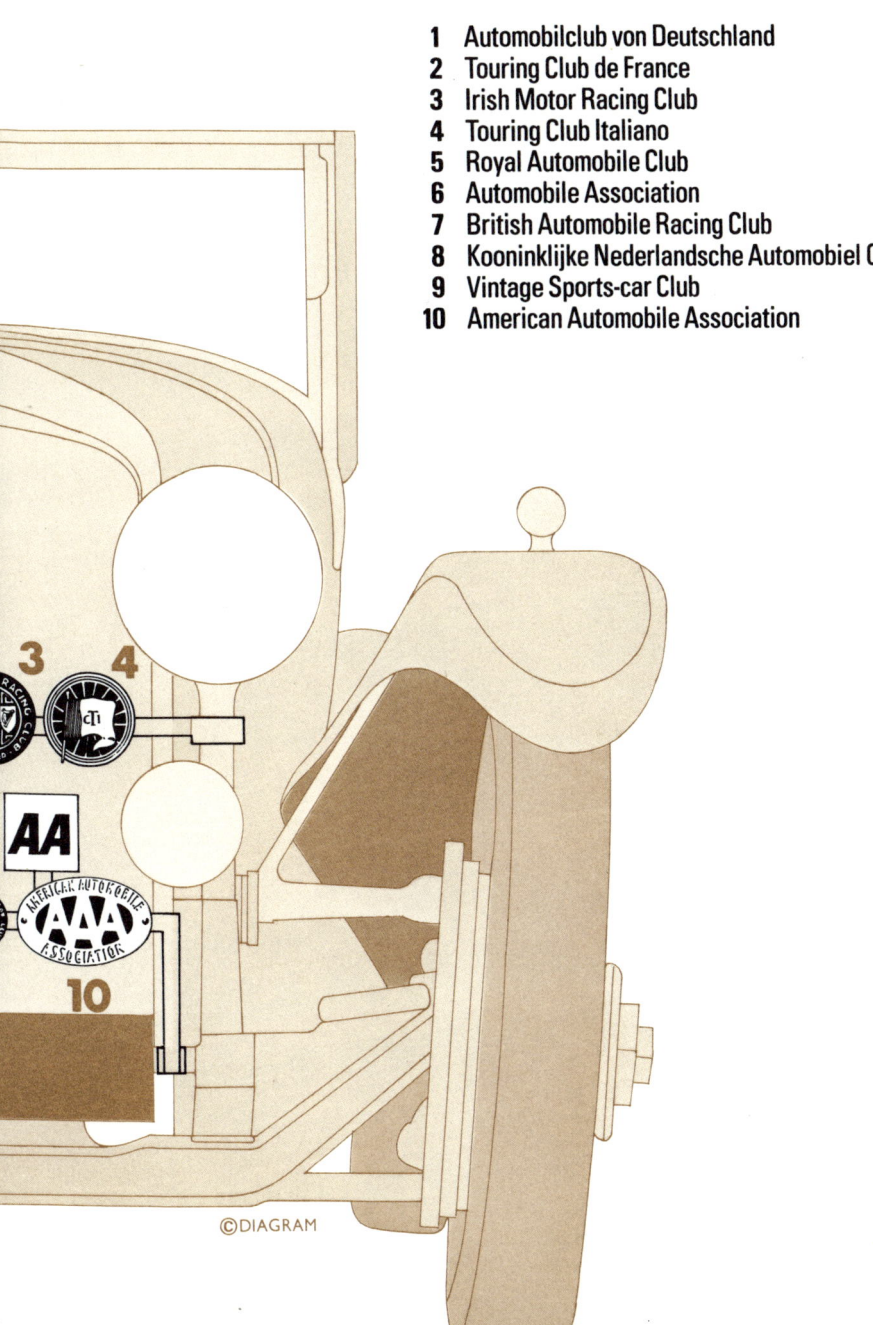

©DIAGRAM

Built for the job

Each of these vehicles does a special job.

Do you know what it is?

1 Road roller presses flat tarmac on the road
2 Shovel truck shifts earth or sand
3 Snow plough clears snow from the road
4 Fork-lift truck lifts crates and boxes
5 Crash truck pulls damaged vehicles
6 Racing car competes in races
7 Road sweeper cleans the road
8 Moon buggy takes astronauts over the moon's surface
9 Land Rover and trailer transport horses
10 Landing craft lands soldiers on beaches

Trees and leaves

Can you find any of the leaves shown at the bottom of the page? Which trees are they from? Why not collect some of them and press them in a scrap book?

1 Horse-chestnut a
2 Sycamore b
3 Silver fir c
4 Ash d
5 Oak e
6 Lime f

Attention! Men at work
Have you ever seen anyone doing these jobs?

1. Hunting
2. Herding sheep
3. Repairing the road
4. Laying cables
5. Repairing telephone wires
6. Cleaning the road
7. Painting white lines
8. Laying paving stones
9. Surveying
10. Inspecting the drains
11. Cleaning lamps
12. Sweeping the streets
13. Helping children cross the road

Plants

These plants often grow in banks and hedges along quiet country roads.
Find as many as you can — but be very careful to keep a look out for traffic.

1 Red poppy
2 Clover
3 Buttercup
4 Dandelion
5 Bluebell
6 Primrose
7 Cow parsley

Birds

Have you ever seen any of these birds? Do you know their names? When you've spotted one of them, write down its name in your spotting book.

42

1 Peregrine falcon
2 Swallow
3 Wren
4 Teal
5 Barn owl
6 Herring gull
7 Raven
8 Heron

43

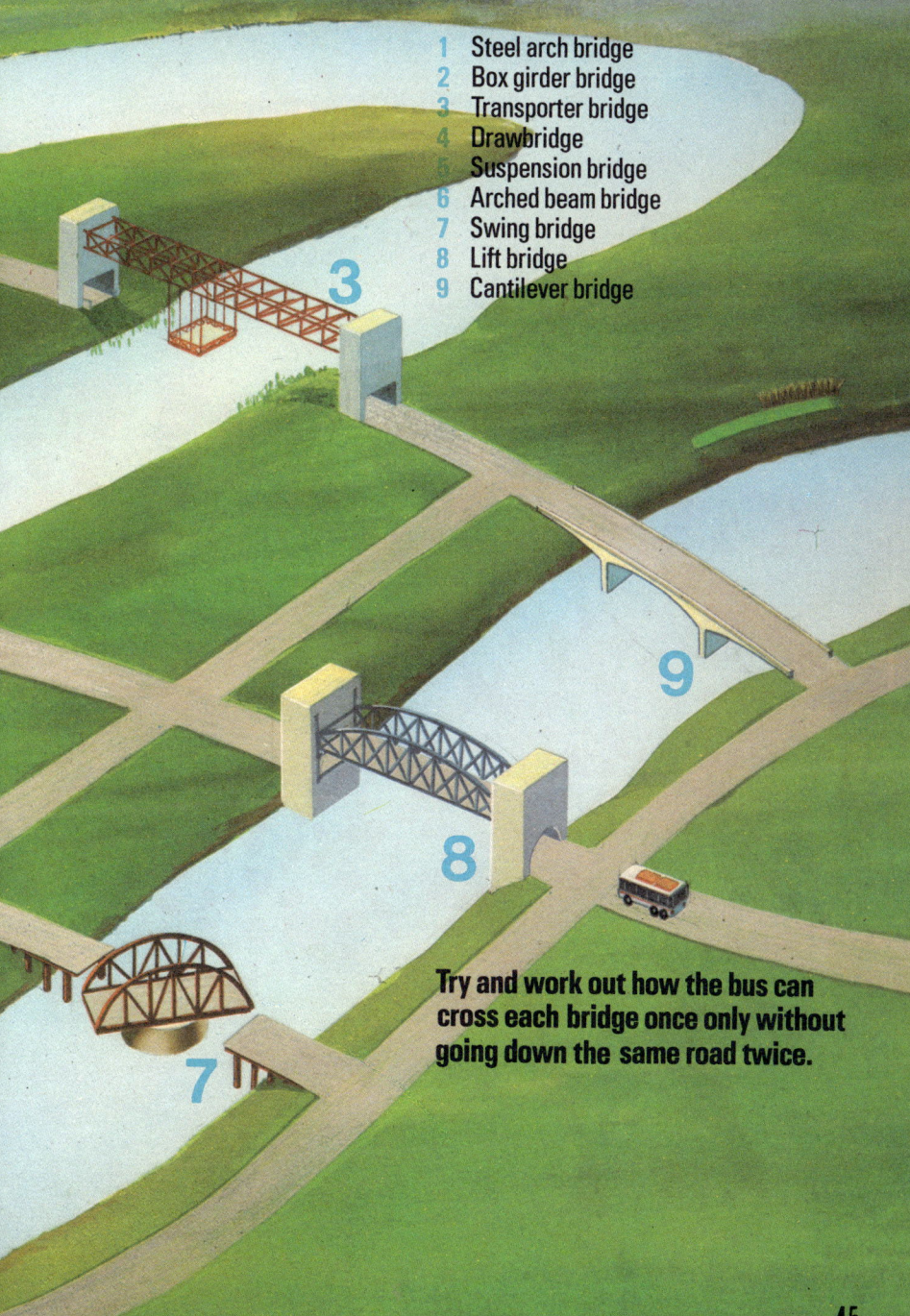